Dad To Be

A 12 Month Action Plan to Guide New Fathers Through Pregnancy

Taylor Cameron

©Copyright 2021 by Cascade Publishing

All rights reserved.

It is not legal to reproduce, duplicate, or transmit any part of this document in either electronic means or in printed format. Recording of this publication is strictly prohibited.

Table of Contents

Introduction 1

Chapter One: Preconception, Preparing For Pregnancy 4

Chapter Two: First Trimester 24

Chapter Three: Second Trimester 44

Chapter Four: Third Trimester 58

Chapter Five: Postpartum, Taking Care Of Your Baby 73

Conclusion 88

Introduction

"Becoming a father, I think it inevitably changes your perspective of life. I don't get nearly enough sleep. And the simplest things in life are completely satisfying. I find you don't have to do as much. Like you don't go on as many outings."

- Hugh Jackman

Congratulations! You're going to be a dad! You are about to witness a miracle that billions before you have experienced. This time, however, the baby is yours.

There is nothing like bringing home your newborn baby, as s/he gently wraps those little hands around one of your fingers. As soon as you walk your baby through those doors, who you are will be changed forever. I have always believed birth and human creation to be one of the most humbling experiences on Earth. Observing this tiny being, who is but days old, it finally dawns on you that this child will need everything inside of you to survive. When s/he scrapes one or both knees and is in tears from shock, as from pain, you will need to tend the wound, then tend the heart. When s/he's hungry and starts a feud with you because ice cream truly is good enough for dinner, you will need to be firm, but kind: broccoli is a better alternative!

Becoming a father will change your relationship to everyone and everything around you. It brings a new level of illumination, understanding, and appreciation for your life, your partner, your family, and so much more words cannot describe. This is a wonderful, exciting period in your life. Your dedication to be prepared is a commendable and honorable choice. You are dedicated to being the best dad that you can be for your child. This book honors your dedication, bringing you a *12 Month Action Plan* to support you through your pregnancy.

Like everything you do, you want to be prepared for fatherhood. Our goal is to bring you practical information for the preconception, prepartum, and postpartum.

In the first month of preconception, this book will guide you on the process of ovulation, fertilization, and conception. It will give you knowledge on your partner's fertile window (the best time for conception), how to track it, and what happens during the process of conception. I will also share with you some of the best health tips to keep in mind when you are planning on having a baby. In addition, you will learn how medication can affect your chances of conception.

This book will break down the nine months of pregnancy, divided into the first, second, and third trimester of pregnancy. It aims to teach you what to expect during every single month, from the milestones to plan for, the questions to ask your doctor, and what you can do to help your partner have a comfortable, healthy pregnancy. Finally, this book will bring you post-partum advice for the two months after birth. You will, no doubt, have a lot of questions once the baby arrives. You may wonder what to feed the baby? How much? How often? What do you do when the baby won't stop crying throughout the night? What happens if the baby is sick?

The last chapter of this book will prepare you for your new baby, so that there are no surprises on your race to becoming a great dad.

Every parent wants the best life for their child. Hence, every piece of advice given in this book is aimed at helping you grow a happy, healthy baby. The first few years are incredibly important for your child's development. Researchers have found that the decisions and experiences that parents make early on affect their child for the rest of their lives. For example, an infant whose mother maintained unhealthy eating practices during pregnancy can obtain a higher chance of developing diabetes and struggling with obesity. I understand that you want to give your child the best head start in life. What better way than to plan conception, prepartum, and postpartum with exceeding care?

I recommend that you mark with a highlighter or some stickers as you read through this book. This will help you bookmark important information for later use. Bookmarking will be a life saver during those moments when you might not remember a particular piece of information pertinent to the occasion.

So, if you're ready, let's begin!

Chapter One:

Preconception, Preparing For Pregnancy

"My biggest achievement—besides being drafted into the NBA—was becoming a father. Being a father has made me experience things that have contributed to my maturity and personal growth."

- Dwayne Wade

It is easy to think of having a baby as a natural cycle of life. Why not? You continue to have plenty of fun together with your partner and, sooner or later, a baby pops out! Preconception is, undeniably, the most fun part of the baby-making process.

However, there are certain responsibilities that arise with the preconception process. Understanding how to prepare for pregnancy will increase your chances of a healthy pregnancy and a healthy baby. You will also need to understand the processes of ovulation, fertilization, and conception to plan a successful conception. Finally, you will need to know how to plan for pregnancy with your partner.

So, strap in, and let's go!

Ovulation, Fertilization & Conception

Ovulation is, quite simply, the female body's means of preparing for new life. The female reproductive system runs like clockwork, in what is known as a menstrual cycle. Every month, the reproductive system releases eggs, ready to be fertilized by sperm.

The menstrual cycle runs on hormones. It repeats itself around every 21 to 35 days or so, beginning with the process of menstruation. The average menstrual cycle lasts approximately 28 days. It begins with the first day of the last period and ends with the first day of the next menstrual period. Here is typically what occurs during a woman's menstrual cycle:

Days One to Five (Follicular Phase)

This is when a woman begins menstruating (usually between 2 to 7 days). While this is happening, the ovaries develop egg-filled follicles, within each follicle a single egg is held. The eggs inside the follicles start developing.

Days Five to Eight (Follicular Phase)

One of the follicles begins to mature, while the rest are absorbed back into the ovary. The body starts preparing for pregnancy by producing more estrogen. The period comes to a halt by day eight and the lining of the uterus begins to thicken. This is how the woman's uterus prepares for a fertilized egg.

Day Fourteen (Ovulation Phase)

The hormone levels are at their highest during the ovulation phase. This is when the body is fully prepared to receive a fertilized egg. The ovary releases the egg, hoping the egg will become fertilized by sperm. Naturally, this the perfect time to perform intercourse with your partner. The egg will survive between 12 to 24 hours after it is released by the body, however there is no rush. A woman has what is called a "fertile window" because sperm can live in a woman's body for up to 5 days after ejaculation. This gives you around 3-4 days before ovulation begins to conceive. To conceive simply means to be successfully impregnated.

Days Fifteen to Twenty-Four (Luteal Phase)

The egg begins to travel through the fallopian tube in the ovulation phase. If sperm is present in the woman's reproductive system it will be fertilized. After fertilization, the egg becomes an embryo and continues its way through the fallopian tube to land on (or embed in) the uterus lining. The uterus lining is where the embryo and the amniotic sac protecting your baby will form.

If the embryo embeds into the uterus lining, then pregnancy has officially begun. Pregnancy usually occurs two or three weeks following the ovulation and fertilization process.

Days Twenty-Four to Twenty-Eight (Luteal Phase)

If the egg does not become fertilized, or if it does fertilize but is unsuccessful at implanting into the uterus, it dissolves at the final stage of the menstrual cycle. Since your partner is not pregnant, her hormone levels will drop rapidly. Usually, this is what causes PMS in some women.

The cycle begins again on day one, and the dissolved egg is released along with the excess uterus lining in what is known as a "period."

Planning for a Baby

Being a dad is a wonderful, life-changing experience. You are about to witness new life learn to walk, talk, sing, be cheeky, and get away with it just by being cute. There is nothing like it!

From the moment your child is conceived, s/he becomes your first responsibility. Although it's the mother that falls pregnant, caring for your baby begins at conception even for the father. There are things you can do to ensure that the baby is well taken care of even while still in the womb. Remember that a child's time in the womb goes on to affect every aspect of their life in the future, from mental health to physiological health to even things like their career aspirations and their relationship with others.

To give your child the best start in life, it is best you plan for a few things before your child arrives. Here are a few pointers:

1. Financial planning

Raising a baby is very expensive. Even if you have insurance, you may still need to pay deductibles every time your partner goes for a check-up. Babies also grow really fast. A three-month-old baby is surprisingly much bigger than a one-week-old baby. You will need new clothes, additional food, extra diapers, and so on. Your partner will also need the most nutritious and healthy food to recover from childbirth. If she is breastfeeding, she will need to eat a healthy diet to ensure that your baby acquires plenty of nutrients. And this is just the beginning. You have a lifetime of taking care of your child's ever-growing needs.

Planning for a baby should, ideally, begin before you conceive a baby. For example, it is a good idea to obtain any vaccines for the mother that she may not have received in the past, such as flu or measles. Pregnant women are also prone to gum disease and oral ill-health and may need to visit the doctor and dentist often. Additionally, your health insurance may not cover your chosen birth plan, meaning that you will have to include birth in your budget. Likewise, your partner may need to take maternity leave. It can also be a great idea to plan for an "emergency fund" in your budget in case of any emergencies.

You must plan deliberately to avoid falling into any financial pitfalls.

2. Good communication with your partner

Having a child with your partner is one of the biggest life decisions you will make. When the baby arrives, you will be too groggy and tired to have important discussions. For instance, how you will approach discipline; how you want to raise your child; or what name you want to give your child. Have those conversations before you start trying for a baby. Where possible, you will want to settle all differences early on, not when you are both struggling with a crying new-born.

During pregnancy, stress is unequivocally bad for both your baby and your partner. Research has shown that prenatal stress "can have significant effects on pregnancy, maternal health and human development across their lifespan". It can cause negative physiological changes to the developing fetus and it can drastically affect the mother's physiological health. Conversely, the mother can pass on her stress hormones to the baby causing "impaired brain development as a result of neurotoxicity". Indeed, psychiatric research concludes that:

> "Maternal psychological distress is a major public health concern and needs timely detection and intervention to prevent any adverse pregnancy outcome. There is ample evidence from literature that justifies

the association of prenatal maternal mental stress and elevated cortisol with delayed infant motor and cognitive development."

Here are a few topics to discuss with your partner before making the decision to conceive a baby:

- Is this the right time for us to have a baby?

    Are our values aligned as a couple? Are we financially, emotionally, and mentally responsible and prepared to have a baby at this point in our lives and in our relationship? Do we both want a baby as a celebration of our love? Does our desire to have a baby come from the right place or will it end up harming our child psychologically?

- What are our expectations as parents and as a couple?

    Having a baby changes your relationship with your partner. You must communicate with your partner about the expectations you have for your postpartum life. What are your hopes and fears about the baby's arrival? For instance, you may fear that the baby will divert too much of your partner's attention from your relationship. How do you want to divide labor in the house once the baby arrives? How will you share the labor of feeding the baby during the night? How involved do you want to be in nurturing your child, whether emotionally, or in any other way?

- Who will work and who will stay at home?

    It is important to discuss the work-home balance between the pair of you. For instance, it might be a case where one partner works part-time, while another works full-time. The dynamics may also change from time to time. What is most important is making sure you are united about your values concerning childcare, home, and work. If you both want to work full-time, can you afford childcare or do you have a relative who is happy to watch the baby while you are both at work? Do you prefer to have one parent taking care of the baby full time in lieu of childcare?

- How should we parent?

Some parents are strict, some are disciplinarian, and some are lenient. You will want to avoid falling into the pattern of one parent being the fun one and the other being the strict one. This causes a big rift between couples. Talk about how you will approach parenthood and discipline to ensure that you present a united front to your child.

What did your parents get right that you want to incorporate into your parenting? What did they get wrong and how would you like to change that with your new baby?

- What values will we teach our child?

This is a very important conversation that can make or break a family. What are the important life, religious, and philosophical values that you want your child to learn? Are they in tune with your partner's? If you have contrasting values, you may have to compromise on which beliefs you will raise your child with. This is a very important conversation that will prevent a lot of heartache in the future.

- Do you have enough strength and dedication for a baby?

An infant consumes a lot of your energy, time, and dedication to raise to adulthood. You will both have less time for each other and for yourself. Are you prepared to make that sacrifice? How will you make time for each other even amidst the chaos of taking care of a baby? How will you ensure that the growing baby does not dim your passion for each other and cause you to grow distant?

- Are we prepared for infertility?

About 13% of women aged 15-49 in the United States have used infertility services. Likewise, more than 13% of women of the same age range suffer from impaired fecundity (having trouble conceiving or carrying a baby to term). Alternatively, 9% of men of reproductive age also struggle with infertility concerns. One in eight couples also struggle to conceive and one in three Americans have sought fertility treatment or know someone who has.

Furthermore, the male partner is more likely the sole cause, or contributing cause, of infertility in about 40% of infertile couples. You and your partner should discuss the potential of infertility or impaired fecundity. In this case, there are other alternatives, such as IVF, surrogacy, and adoption. Each alternative has its advantages and disadvantages, as well as its philosophical considerations. They are also very emotionally and financially taxing and, sometimes, can remain unsuccessful. If one or both of you are infertile, you will need to rely on each other for support throughout the ordeal, as this process can tear a couple apart. Remember to stay positive and supportive through this process as it can be quite hard to stomach for some.

3. Your lifestyle

The most important question to ask yourself as a dad-to-be is if you are ready to have a baby. Are you ready to wake up early for the foreseeable future to make pancakes for your child? Are you mentally healthy enough to truly be an aware, present father? These days, fatherhood is celebrated more and more. This is a good thing, of course. Gone are the days when fathers were represented as fools who couldn't be trusted with their own babies. So, are you ready to step up into this responsibility? This is the most difficult and most rewarding thing that you will ever do. Children with physically and emotionally present fathers have been scientifically proven to do much better than children without them.

Having a child means sacrificing parts of your former lifestyle. Whether you are a gamer, a fisherman, a travel junkie, a runner, a gym buff, or anything else you like to pursue as a hobby, this will now always take second place to being a father. Sure, you can still enjoy these activities, but your child quickly becomes your first priority.

Fertility

Your health is just as vital as the mother's health when trying to conceive. Whatever you ingest will affect your sperm and you want the best quality and highest sperm count to produce the healthiest baby possible. Your overall wellbeing is also imperative. Your lifestyle choices will drastically affect your chances for conception. Poor lifestyle choices can result in a reduced libido. Less sex will, in turn, result in fewer offspring. Similarly, diet and stress will also change your sperm's genetic construction. Indeed, scientists have found out that:

"The legacy of a dad's behavior can even live on in his child if his epigenetic elements enter an embryo. For instance, mice born to fathers that experience stress can inherit the behavioral consequences of traumatic memories. Additionally, mouse dads with less-than-desirable diets can pass a wonky metabolism onto their kids."

The following lifestyle choices may affect the quality and quantity of your sperm:

- Alcohol, especially chronic alcohol use
- Cigarettes
- Age
- Recreational drugs, such as marijuana
- Medical drugs
- Toxic material in the environment, such as lead, pesticides, and plastic
- Hormonal imbalances
- Stress
- Anabolic steroids
- Radiation treatment and chemotherapy
- Health issues and medical problems

Chronic Diseases

If you or your partner suffer from a chronic health condition or complication that prevents you from partaking in a healthy pregnancy, it is best to speak to your doctor before conception. Many individuals with chronic diseases are required to take strong medications. Some medications could be harmful to your embryo/fetus. Some risks include placing the fetus' life at risk, stillbirth, premature birth, developmental problems, birth defects, and mental health disorders.

Pregnancy can also severely harm a woman with a chronic condition. It may worsen her symptoms, cause her severe, debilitating pain, or put her life at risk.

If you or your partner have any of the following conditions, speak to your doctor about any risks or queries you may have before making the decision to conceive a child:

- Obesity
- Diabetes
- Depression
- Lupus
- HIV/AIDS
- Thyroid
- Asthma
- Multiple sclerosis
- Bipolar disorder
- Cardiovascular disease
- Rheumatoid arthritis
- Chronic pain
- High blood pressure
- Obsessive-compulsive disease

If your partner has one or more chronic health conditions, she may require the services of specialized doctors during and after pregnancy. You and your partner will need to consider the financial costs of such a pregnancy, especially if your insurance does not cover any of these services. Additionally, you will need to consider the costs of taking care of a baby and infant with possible birth or developmental deficiencies.

What to Eat

Although scientific research has typically focused on what a woman should eat to improve and increase her fertility, a growing number of research is showing that the male diet is very important for fertility and baby health. It is best to start eating healthy, nutrient-dense food before conception. This will keep your body in great shape, making conception easier. It will also decrease the chance of your baby developing birth defects as a result of low-quality sperm. Some really good food to eat to increase your sperms vitality include:

- Zinc-Rich Food

   Oysters have a higher zinc content than any other food; they are also a known aphrodisiac. They have been linked to sperm motility (the sperm's ability to move efficiently to reach the egg) and increased semen volume. Other foods that are high in zinc are nuts, eggs, beans, whole grains, poultry, beef, and dairy products. You may also speak with your doctor about taking a daily multivitamin that is high in zinc.

- Antioxidant-Rich Food

   Foods rich in antioxidants (including nuts, turmeric, berries, dark chocolate, beets, kale, and spinach) protect sperm from cellular damage and increase sperm motility. Pomegranate juice is high in antioxidants and has been proven to boost the quality of sperm.

- Vitamin E & Vitamin C-Rich Food

   Foods rich in vitamin E (like mangoes, spinach, and avocados) and vitamin C (like oranges, pineapples, and tomatoes) are also linked to a slight increase in sperm motility. Sweet potatoes contain both vitamin C and vitamin E.

- Omega-3 Fatty Acids-Rich Food

    Omega-3 fatty acid-rich foods (such as oily fish, flax seed, chia seeds, and walnuts) are also known for improving sperm motility and quantity. Omega-3 fatty acids will also improve the blood flow to your genitals, improving your stamina in the bedroom.

- Folate-Rich Foods

    Research has found that men with low levels of folate have an increased risk of having sperm containing too many or too few chromosomes. Too many or too few chromosomes can cause miscarriages and birth defects. Foods that contain folate (leafy-green vegetables, chickpeas, lentils, beans, and fruits) help prevent genetic abnormalities in your baby, passed on from your sperm.

- Maca Root

    Maca root is a very well-known aphrodisiac. It boosts libido for both men and women.

A woman's diet is very important when she is trying to conceive. It reduces the chances of birth defects, such as spina bifida, and the chances of your partner developing pregnancy complications, such as preeclampsia (high blood pressure, protein in urine and swollen legs, feet, and hands).

Here are some great dietary options for a woman to eat when she is trying to get pregnant:

- Folate-Rich Foods

    Folate (vitamin B9) is the most important vitamin a woman needs to consume if she wants to become pregnant. It is recommended that she take 400 micrograms of folate per day for a month before trying to conceive. Folate is very essential for the development of healthy baby cells and the prevention of serious birth defects, such as spina bifida (when the spine and spinal cord don't form properly).

Folate is present in leafy vegetables, such as spinach, broccoli, kale, and Swiss chard, oranges, strawberries, folate-enriched cereals, nuts, and beans. It may be difficult to reach optimal levels from daily diet alone, so a supplement is always recommended. In fact, after your first prenatal checkup, your doctor will prescribe you folate to ensure that your baby develops properly.

- Magnesium & Calcium-Rich Foods

    Scientists have found that magnesium and calcium are crucial for female preconception. Foods high in magnesium include legumes, such as beans, leafy vegetables, dark chocolate, seeds and nuts, and fiber-rich whole grains, such as quinoa and dairy foods. Sources of calcium include beans, lentils, almonds, rhubarb, whey protein, and dairy foods.

- Iron-Rich Foods

    An iron deficiency in a pregnant woman can result in an underweight or premature baby. A woman's daily iron intake will need to increase from 18 mg to 27 mg once she falls pregnant. Eating lean poultry meats like turkey is a great source of iron. Other meats such as red meat and chicken are also perfect substitutes. In addition, liver meat is a great source of iron if your partner can stomach it.

    Vegetable sources like beets, spinach, collard greens, peas, and sweet potatoes can also contain iron. Some breads and cereals are also iron-fortified. Finally, beans and lentils are known for their iron content, as are some fruits, like watermelon, raisins, prunes, and strawberries.

- Fiber-Rich Foods

    Women planning to get pregnant should increase their fiber intake from 25 grams per day to 35 grams per day. An increase in complex, slowly digestible carbs will keep her feeling full for longer. She will need to eat plenty of whole grains, beans, legumes, fruits, and vegetables to increase fiber intake.

- Omega-3 Fatty Acids-Rich Foods

    Omega-3 fatty acids will increase blood flow to a woman's reproductive organs. It also regulates hormones that induce ovulation. The oils in food like cod liver oil, walnuts, and avocados can replace the unhealthy fats found in processed food.

- Protein-Rich Foods

    Protein is a key macro-nutrient for female fertility. Without enough protein, a woman will have less frequent menstrual periods, disrupting her ovulation cycle. In fact, without enough protein, a pregnant woman risks early miscarriage. The recommended daily amount of protein for a woman is 45 grams to 50 grams. This should increase to around 60 grams to 65 grams once a woman is pregnant.

What to Avoid

Conversely, there are certain foods that will increase your infertility and reduce your sperm quality. They include the following:

- Junk Food

    Fried, fatty, and sugary foods have been scientifically proven to reduce the quality of sperm. In fact, a standard American diet has been linked with low sperm count, while a healthy and nutritious diet has been linked with healthy sperm.

- High-Fat Dairy Food

  High-fat and full-fat dairy is associated with bad sperm motility, low sperm count, and abnormal sperm shape. It is better to consume low-fat dairy instead, which is associated with better sperm quality.

- Processed Red Meats

  Processed red meats, like hot dogs, sausages, and deli meats, are all linked to a low sperm count and bad semen quality.

- Soy Products

  Soy is a very controversial food in the world of nutrition. Research continues to determine the impact of soy on our health, but some studies have shown a link between soy and low sperm count.

- Alcohol

  Consuming alcohol above the recommended intake has been linked to a low sperm count and bad quality semen. On the other hand, when men stop their excessive alcohol intake, the effects are only partially reversible.

- Caffeine

  Research findings on caffeine's effect on sperm is mixed. Some research has shown a decrease in sperm quality when caffeine is consumed; this is true about excessive amounts of caffeine in particular. Other research has shown that moderate caffeine consumption is good for sperm. To be on the safe side, keep your caffeine consumption at a low-moderate level.

- High Mercury Content Fish

    Fish that are high in mercury, such as swordfish, marlin, king mackerel and bigeye tuna, have been linked to infertility in both men and women.

Abuse

Many women are often first abused by their partner when they become pregnant, according to the American College of Obstetricians and Gynecologists. Three of the most common triggers that cause a spouse to become abusive are:

- Being upset if it was an unplanned pregnancy. Feeling "trapped."

- Feeling stressed and anxious because you have to financially support your first baby or another baby.

- Feeling jealous that your partner's attention is now centered around the baby and not you.

One of the considerations for preparing to have a child is to ask yourself if you are truly ready to have a baby. You must consider not only financial preparation, but the mental and emotional preparation as well. Bad parents are often mentally and emotionally traumatized individuals. Have you done the internal work needed to be a good parent? Have you processed the traumas you suffered as a child and even a young adult? Do you suffer from PTSD? Sometimes PTSD does not manifest in our lives until we are triggered. Do you still struggle with the relationship you have with your parents? Do you understand how to truly love your partner without need, codependence, shame, blame, fear, or anxiety?

Before you become a dad, it is highly advisable that you have completed some form of therapy and can answer the above questions with a confident "yes." If not, you may hand down the traumas that your caregivers passed on to you to your partner or your child in a cycle known as "generational trauma." If your partner is already pregnant as you are reading this book, it is not too late to start therapy. Nor is it to be looked at in a negative limelight. Therapy is a great resource to help any individual to open up, deal with or uncover any unrealized traumas, or even to just talk through any difficulties. Don't feel ashamed. Therapy is great.

If your partner is abusive, or, if she displays some of the signs of an abuser below, you should seek therapy before you decide to have a baby. Despite the cultural myth that only men abuse women, men can be the ones who are abused as well. Moreover, having a baby with an abusive partner is an almost certain guarantee that your partner will also abuse your child. It is best to seek professional advice to overcome any of these concerns.

Signs you may be in an abusive relationship include:

- Constantly raised voices
- Being ignored and stonewalled
- Forcibly avoiding your friends and family at the request of your partner
- Being told or made to feel like you are the cause of all the problems in the relationship
- Gaslighting or being told that only your partner's point of view is correct
- Unpredictable mood swings making you walk on eggshells
- Continuously being attacked in every conversation, making you have to defend yourself at all times

- Being controlled and manipulated by your partner telling you they will leave you if you do anything they do not approve of

- Being disrespected in most conversations you have with them

- Receiving hate and ridicule for being yourself

- Constant possessiveness and jealousy; cheating accusations

- Humiliating and degrading you in front of others

- Physical abuse

- Threatening to call the cops about made-up accusations (e.g., sexual assault or violence)

It is absolutely important to seek help if you feel that you are in an abusive relationship. Speak to a doctor, a therapist, a counsellor, or a trusted friend or family member. Speak up.

Chapter Summary

- Understanding how to prepare for pregnancy will increase your chances of a healthy pregnancy and a healthy baby.

- Being a dad is a wonderful, life-changing experience.

- Planning for a baby should, ideally, begin before you conceive a baby.

- Having a baby is very expensive. You must plan deliberately to avoid falling into any financial pitfalls.

- Your health is just as important as the mother's health when trying to conceive. It is best to start eating healthy, nutrient-dense food before conception.

- Before you become a dad, it is highly advisable that you have completed some form of therapy.

- If your partner is abusive, or you suspect that your partner may be abusive, you should seek therapy or professional help.

In the next chapter you will learn how to prepare for the first trimester of pregnancy.

Chapter Two:

First Trimester

"Never is a man more of a man than when he is the father of a newborn."

- Matthew McConaughey

Once you receive news of your partners pregnancy, congratulations are in order! This is a momentous direction that your life has taken. No doubt, you feel proud, accomplished, and full of life. What's more masculine than becoming a father? So, what's next for you?

Your partner will now be in the first trimester. The first trimester is when the baby is still in the earliest stages of development. Many pregnancies do not even show signs in the first trimester because the embryo is still too small, measuring about 2½ inches. For first time mothers, a pregnancy will begin to show between weeks 12 and 16. Whereas, if it is not her first time, a woman may start to show earlier. In fact, the doctor counts the start of a woman's last period as the first week of pregnancy. In the first trimester, the placenta (a pancake-like organ that feeds the baby nutrients and oxygen) begins to develop. The placenta also carries waste away from the baby to the mother, who then eliminates it.

Likewise, the amniotic sac and fluid begin to develop too. They protect the baby from being harmed by outside forces. The amniotic fluid contains antibodies, nutrients, and hormones that keep your baby in top condition.

By week six, important organs, such as your baby's heart, will begin to form. By week 12, the intestines and the nose will have fully formed. Other organs and body parts, like the genitalia, face and arms are still forming. You may be wondering why everything seems so disjointed at this point. This is because different parts form at different stages. Some limbs, like the arms, take many weeks to fully form. Although babies are known for being cute, they certainly do not start out in the womb that way.

Your First Prenatal Visit

As soon as you find out that you and your partner are pregnant, you will both need to book her first prenatal appointment. The next 8 to 9 months are going to take its toll on her physical and mental health, so you will need to be very supportive. The easier you make it on her, the happier you both will be.

The first prenatal visit typically takes place eight weeks after your partner's last menstrual period. During this visit, the doctor will tell you the baby's expected delivery date. Your doctor will also ask you if you want to do a "first-trimester screening". This screening checks if your baby potentially has genetic complications, like Down syndrome.

Your first prenatal visit is very important for the health of your baby. Your healthcare practitioner will ask you and your partner very detailed medical questions about your health and genetic history. They will want to know if there is a history of medical problems or mental health problems on either side of the child's parentage. Furthermore, they will want to know your history with medication, as well as your partner's history. This can play an important role during your child's formation in the womb. Lastly, be prepared to answer questions about your lifestyle. Do you consume alcohol and caffeine? How often, if at all, do you smoke? Do you use recreational drugs? Have you traveled to destinations where certain infections, like the Zika virus, are common?

The doctor or OB/GYN may also carry out a blood test on your partner. The blood test checks her blood type; measures her level of hemoglobin (to check for anemia); checks for infections that are dangerous for your baby's health, such as HIV, syphilis, chlamydia, and hepatitis B; and checks that she has immunity to infections like measles and chickenpox. If your partner is already vaccinated for these diseases, she should bring proof of her vaccinations with her to the check-up. In addition, a urine sample test is very likely to be carried out. Pregnant women have a higher chance of developing a UTI because of changes in their hormones, uterus, and immune system. If left untreated, a UTI can seriously harm your baby by causing preterm labor (going into labor when your baby has not yet reached its due date).

It is very important to go to this screening with your partner. Both of you can speak with your doctor about your partner's birth plan. A birth plan is exactly what it sounds like. Births are typically pre-planned. Of course, they are often chaotic and may not go according to plan, but that is exactly why you need a birth plan. Think of it as a football game. No two games are the same, but every coach still needs an offensive strategy and a defensive strategy. Strategies may change during the game, but it is still better to have a pre-planned strategy to avoid surprises.

The birth plan will discuss whether your partner wants an epidural or not. It will also discuss breastfeeding; what type of delivery your partner wants (for example, home delivery, water delivery, and so on); the people she wants in her delivery room and any other contingencies.

Questions to Ask Your Doctor

You will, no doubt, have many questions during your first visit. It may be a bit more challenging to think about questions as the father, since pregnancy is still centered very heavily around the woman's experience. You can try spending a few days thinking about what questions you may have. Women are also often encouraged to write down any question so as to avoid forgetting. Here are a few questions to start you off:

- Can we have sex or are there any pregnancy complications that may keep her from having sex?
- Can she still work? Are there any complications that may keep her from working?
- What are some signs to look for that signal an emergency? What do I do in the case of an emergency?
- How do I plan financially for delivery? Do I need to speak with the hospital or my insurance agent?
- Are there any local or online support groups for first-time fathers? Are there any support groups I can talk to when I am feeling overwhelmed?

- What are your suggestions (or referrals) for quitting a harmful substance that I am addicted to, e.g., cigarettes?

- Can my partner continue to take her prescribed medication during pregnancy?

Lifestyle

If you, your partner, or the both of you, smoke, drink, or take recreational drugs, you must tell the doctor. A father's lifestyle choices are just as important as the mother's. As previously mentioned, studies have shown that poor lifestyle choices can reduce the quality of your sperm.

Your partner will need to give up all of these things for the sake of the baby's health. Rest assured, if she is addicted to any of these substances, she will not be asked to go cold turkey. Instead, the doctor will put her on a medical plan to wean her off slowly. At the same time, you may want to think about giving these things up for the sake of your partner. Watching you enjoy a glass of wine while she struggles to keep meals down is not going to boost her morale. Indeed, it will very likely cause friction between you. Likewise, smoking or using recreational drugs around your pregnant wife is a big no-no. Be honest with your doctor about these issues. They will be able to give you confidential advice on how best to address any concerns.

For the next 24 to 36 months, you will have to put your partner first in most of your decisions. Remember that pregnancy, childbirth, and breastfeeding have serious physical, mental, and emotional repercussions on a woman. Apart from the trauma of a stillbirth, a preterm labor, an overdue labor, and other complications that can occur in pregnancy, a woman with a healthy pregnancy will still go through many more complications. Below is a list of some of the complications and side effects that you should expect:

- Hemorrhoids
- Exhaustion and extreme fatigue
- Nausea and vomiting (some women deal with this throughout their pregnancy and are unable to keep any food down)
- Mild to severe abdominal cramps
- Hair loss
- Increased facial/body hair
- Increased blood pressure
- Yeast infections
- Changes in appetite and sense of taste and smell
- Cravings
- Indigestion and heartburn
- Bleeding gums
- Weight gain and redistribution (sometimes permanent)
- Constipation
- Diarrhea
- Bloating, fluid retention, and swelling
- Dizziness and light-headedness
- Acne and other mild skin disorders, such as skin discoloration of the face and abdomen

- Back pain, ranging from mild to severe; some women develop permanent back injuries
- Insomnia and poor sleep
- Congested or bloody nose
- Headaches and migraines
- Pica (an eating disorder characterized by cravings for non-food items)
- Breast pain and embarrassing breast discharges and leakage
- Incontinence and frequent urination
- Swelling of joints, leg cramps, joint pain
- Difficulty and pain when sitting, standing, and bending down
- Shortness of breath
- Anemia
- Depression (prepartum and postpartum)
- Anxiety
- Immune suppression, making women more susceptible to serious and potentially fatal diseases, such as bacterial vaginosis
- Gestational diabetes
- Inability to perform everyday tasks
- Extreme pain before and during childbirth
- Trauma from complicated childbirth, including major surgery, such as a C-section

- Extended postpartum exhaustion and recovery, sometimes taking up to a year to fully recover

- Stretch marks and loose skin; in some cases, severe scarring

- Diastasis recti (permanent abdominal muscle stretch and weakness that can cause problems in everyday life)

- Vaginal muscle weakness

- Pelvic floor disorder (causing discomfort, urinary and rectal incontinence, and reduced quality of life)

- Sagging or larger breasts

- Increase in foot size

- Varicose veins

- Scarring from surgery

- Loss of dental and bone calcium

- Higher lifetime risk of developing Alzheimer's disease

- Embolism (blood clots)

First Trimester Symptoms

The first trimester symptoms are a challenge for the mother. Her hormones are shifting rapidly, causing fluctuations in her mood and prompt physiological changes. A lot of symptoms of the first trimester will usually show up before the mother takes a pregnancy test or visits the doctor. They are symptoms that the body is adapting in preparation for birth. Once you or your partner notice these symptoms, then your partner may want to take a pregnancy test.

Some of the symptoms she will experience include:

- Morning Sickness

    Nausea and vomiting are common symptoms during the first trimester. Morning sickness usually begins between weeks 1 and 4. It is caused by rapidly fluctuating hormones in the woman's body. Although it is labelled as morning sickness, it can happen at any time during the day.

    Your partner can relieve nausea by making sure she does not have an empty stomach. It is best to eat in small amounts every one to two hours, chewing and eating slowly. During pregnancy, a woman usually has cravings for certain foods, whilst also feeling repulsed by other foods. It is best for the mother to avoid foods and smells that worsen her nausea. Ginger is well-known for its anti-nausea properties and can prevent morning sickness and nausea.

    If your partner's queasiness continues throughout day, it is advised that you visit a healthcare practitioner.

- Fatigue, Excessive Sleepiness, & Dizziness

    A pregnant woman in the first trimester will very likely suffer from excessive lethargy due to hormonal changes. It can begin as early as the first week of conception. Usually, it tapers off by the second trimester, only to return by the third trimester.

    When a woman becomes pregnant, her Corpus Luteum (a cyst on her ovary) begins to produce an increased level of progesterone. Progesterone is responsible for many functions during and after pregnancy, including building and sustaining the lining of the uterus, which nourishes the growing baby during the first few weeks of conception. It also prevents the uterus from contracting during pregnancy, leading to premature birth or miscarriage and causes the mother to produce more milk glands, needed for breastfeeding after childbirth.

A very important hormone, progesterone is absolutely essential for the embryo's health during pregnancy. Since the hormone is at high levels in a pregnant woman, it can lead to fatigue and drowsiness.

The baby is also constantly growing during the first trimester, becoming bigger and heavier. This means that the mother is carrying an increasingly heavier load every day, further causing her fatigue. This is combined with pumping extra blood to supply the baby with oxygen and nutrients.

The body goes through serious changes during pregnancy. A woman in the first trimester will often feel weak and sleepy because her metabolism is now running faster while her blood pressure and blood sugar are lower. She is using more nutrients and water than normal to power her body and her heart rate is up. Think of it as connecting another house to the generator powering your house. Your generator will need more gas, more maintenance, and more check-ups due to the increased load.

- Breast swelling & tenderness

Swollen and tender breasts are typically an early sign of pregnancy in a woman. As soon as a zygote (very recently fertilized egg) implants in the uterus, the body begins to release increased levels of estrogen and progesterone. These hormones are responsible for breast swelling and tenderness, as they prepare the body for lactation and breastfeeding.

Estrogen stimulates the breast duct cells to grow. In addition, it activates the secretion of prolactin, a hormone that causes the breasts to enlarge and begin producing milk. After birth, a woman's estrogen and progesterone levels will drop rapidly, while prolactin levels increase. As a result, lactation is triggered. Postpartum decline in estrogen and progesterone levels gives your partner a higher chance of developing postpartum depression and sadness.

- Frequent urination

    Frequent urination is an early sign of pregnancy in a woman. It usually begins around the second to fourth week. It usually declines in the second trimester, only to begin again in the third trimester.

- Implantation bleeding

    This is another early sign of pregnancy. Implantation bleeding is typically a light bleeding or spotting that usually occurs around 10 to 14 days after conception. It is usually accompanied by lower back pain, mood swings, light or faint cramping, headaches, and other first trimester symptoms.

Food

There are certain foods that a pregnant woman cannot consume. A pregnancy-friendly diet will keep the baby safe and healthy during growth. Certain foods can cause developmental disorders, miscarriages, or even death. Moreover, you may need to go food shopping for your partner during the pregnancy. Oftentimes, she may feel too tired, too weak, too sick, too nauseous, or too dizzy to go out to buy food. You may also have to prepare her meals when her symptoms make it difficult for her to function well. As such, it is important to know what foods a pregnant woman should avoid, so that you do not accidentally feed them to your partner. These foods are:

- Deli meats

    Deli meats can sometimes be contaminated with listeria. Listeria is a bacterium that can be found in unpasteurized milk and food made from unpasteurized milk, uncooked vegetables, and processed foods. Listeria can cause a miscarriage and premature delivery. If it crosses the placenta, from the mother to the baby, it may infect the baby. This could be life-threatening for both the baby and the mother.

    Even worse, listeria is twenty times more infectious among pregnant women than the general population. Approximately 22% of perinatal listeriosis cases in fetuses lead to neonatal death or stillbirth.

- Caffeine

    Caffeine has been proven to affect embryo development and even epigenetic inheritance. Research has shown that:

    "Caffeine exposure during sensitive windows of pregnancy may induce epigenetic changes in the developing fetus or even the germ cells to cause adult-onset diseases in subsequent generations".

    Further research also reveals that pregnant women who drink more than two caffeinated drinks daily during the first seven weeks of pregnancy are at a high risk of miscarriage. It is best to avoid caffeine intake because it may also lead to miscarriage in the first trimester. In fact, research has proven that the preconception consumption of caffeine by both partners increases a mother's risk for miscarriage post conception. Researchers at Ohio State University found that "A woman is more likely to miscarry if she and her partner drink more than two caffeinated beverages a day during the weeks leading up to conception".

Caffeine consumption in pregnant mothers has also been linked to withdrawal symptoms in infants, premature birth, and low birth weight. Caffeine also causes the mother's body to eliminate fluids, causing both calcium and water loss. A pregnant woman should avoid caffeine, just to be safe. She should replace it with water; no added sugar, non-caffeinated tea; and milk.

- Alcohol

There is no safe amount of alcohol to consume during pregnancy and breastfeeding. Alcohol intake during pregnancy can also lead to fetal alcohol syndrome, as well as other developmental disorders.

- Unwashed vegetables

Toxoplasmosis is a parasite that can be found on unwashed vegetables. It is usually found in soil, infecting unwashed vegetables through contact. If you are infected with toxoplasmosis, you can pass it on to your baby, causing eye and brain developmental issues in the fetus.

- Raw meat & seafood

Raw meat and raw seafood may infect you with toxoplasmosis, coliform bacteria, or salmonella. These infections can be serious and life-threatening for your fetus.

- Soft cheeses & unpasteurized milk

A pregnant woman may be infected with listeria after eating soft cheeses like brie or Roquefort cheese. Similarly, your partner may get infected with listeria by drinking unpasteurized milk.

- Raw eggs

  Eating raw eggs can cause salmonella. It is rare for a mother to transfer salmonella infection to her fetus. When it does happen, however, it is deadly for the fetus and can lead to miscarriage. You will need to check that foods like mayonnaise, ice cream, custards and other products made from eggs are not made with raw, unpasteurized eggs.

- Fish with mercury

  Pregnant women should avoid fish that contains high levels of mercury, such as king mackerel and swordfish. Mercury may cause developmental delays and brain damage in fetuses. Avoid sushi made with uncooked fish, or sushi made with fish that contains high levels of mercury. The following fish with high levels of mercury used in sushi include:

  - Ahi (yellowfin tuna)
  - Aji (horse mackerel)
  - Buri (adult yellowtail)
  - Hamachi (young yellowtail)
  - Inada (very young yellowtail)
  - Kanpachi (very young yellowtail)
  - Katsuo (bonito)
  - Kajiki (swordfish)
  - Maguro (bigeye, bluefin or yellowfin tuna)
  - Makjiki (blue marlin)

- Meji (young bigeye, bluefin or yellowfin tuna)
- Saba (mackerel)
- Sawara (Spanish mackerel)
- Shiro (albacore tuna)
- Seigo (young sea bass)
- Suzuki (sea bass)
- Toro (bigeye, bluefin or yellowfin tuna)

You should also avoid fish from contaminated water sources. It is best to avoid fish derived from local lakes and rivers, such as striped bass, pike, bluefish, walleye, salmon, and trout. Before you eat any local fish, contact your local health department or the Environmental Protection Agency (EPA) to find out which fish in your local water area is safe to eat throughout pregnancy.

- Freshly squeezed juice

  A pregnant woman should avoid freshly squeezed juice because it is often unpasteurized. Unpasteurized juice can infect her with E. coli and salmonella. Always check the bottle and cartons of juice to make sure that it is not unpasteurized.

- Raw sprouts

  Raw sprouts (which include radishes, clovers, and alfalfa) may contain bacteria like E. coli, salmonella, and listeria in their seeds. E. coli often causes diarrhea, resulting in the mother losing bodily fluids. This may cause dehydration, leading to low amniotic fluid. This could trigger the mother to begin bleeding heavily and go into premature delivery or have a miscarriage or stillbirth.

Support

Paternal support is crucial for a healthy pregnancy, a healthy mother, a healthy birth, and a healthy baby.

Low partner support is associated with smoking, depression, and anxiety. By contrast, "paternal support during pregnancy is considered a predictor of positive birth outcomes". Your support will play a big part in reducing your partner's stress during pregnancy. As you're most likely aware, pregnancy is a very trying time for a woman. She is undergoing a significant amount of physiological and psychological changes. At the same time, she must take care of her body and her health, undergo many medical appointments, exercise, eat healthily, prepare the home for the baby's arrival and, in some cases, work. Your support will greatly help alleviate her stress.

As a matter of fact, your support is equally important for the baby. Remember that stress hormones can pass from the mother to the fetus. Indeed, scientists have found that fetal exposure to excessive stress hormones in the womb is linked to adult mood disorders. Not only that, but overexposure to cortisol in the womb can lead to psychopathy in adulthood.

Secondarily, your support empowers your partner to feel in control of the birth experience. Although the mother might be carrying the fetus, your support during her pregnancy is just as important for the both of you, and for the family. In fact, research states that:

Partner support and perceptions of partner support throughout the pregnancy, birth, and postpartum experience can help reduce stress, help mothers feel in control of their birth experience, reduce postpartum pathologies, strengthen the mother-partner relationship, and therefore strengthen the bond between parents and offspring.

Postpartum pathology can be a factor in insecure mother-offspring attachment, and can affect the mother-partner relationship.

Stress during pregnancy can also lead to poor health decisions including smoking cigarettes, consuming alcohol, and eating unhealthy foods.

You can support your partner in the following ways:

1. Adopting her lifestyle

   It may be difficult for your partner to watch you drink alcohol, smoke, and eat food that she is unable to eat. You can empower her by adopting her lifestyle as best as you can. This will make her feel seen and appreciated and give her the emotional support she needs to practice a healthy lifestyle for the baby's health. There may be days when she needs encouragement to eat something healthy rather than a chocolate bar, or to go for a walk even though she doesn't feel like it. Making her a delicious salad and offering to go on a walk with her will make all the difference in her physical and psychological health.

2. Helping her practice self-care

   Your partner will not be able to achieve a lot of what would normally be simple tasks for herself, especially as she reaches the second and third trimester. For example, she may not be able to draw a bath or give herself a pedicure. Performing and expressing some self-care toward your partner will help her feel relaxed and wash any stress away. Give her massages regularly, especially back and feet massages. As the baby grows bigger, she will be carrying a lot more weight in these two areas. Some women do not like to be massaged during labor, however. Just be mindful and work around your partner as best as possible.

3. Being patient

   It is very likely that your partner's behavior and moods will become irrational and fluctuate briskly. For example, she might ask you to buy her a particular food late at night, only to declare that she can't eat it, or she might snap at you for something innocuous. This is not her fault, neither is it something she can control. A pregnant woman goes through many hormonal changes to nurture the fetus. Be patient with your partner. This also means that you may need to take time away for yourself too. A round of golf or a run in the park will give you time away from your partner to de-stress and to spend quality time alone. It will also give your partner time alone to spend with the baby. As the fetus develops, it loves to hear voices, and especially the mother's voice. This is one of the first bonding experiences between the mother and child.

4. Quality time with her

   Through all the business of a pregnancy, you still need to spend quality time with your partner. Making this a practice will make it easier for you to continue on in a healthy relationship even after the baby arrives. Your partner needs to know that you still find her desirable and beautiful despite her changing body. Many women feel unattractive during pregnancy because of their body adapting to accommodate for the birth. They also feel pressure to lose all the weight gained immediately after pregnancy and to make sure they show no side effects of the pregnancy anywhere else on their bodies. Your partner may feel dejected at the sight of her changing body, so it is important to compliment her and spend romantic time with her. You can also use this time to plan a getaway or do something adventurous (and pregnancy-friendly) before the baby arrives.

You should also spend time together as parents. You can talk to your baby in the womb, read a book, or play some music for the baby. In addition, you can talk about baby names and research baby and toddler care together. Spending quality time with your partner assures her that you love the baby that you created together and that you love her. It is good to create this bond as partners and parents because this will keep both of you feeling connected after birth, even in trying times when the baby will not stop crying and you both haven't slept for days.

5. Going to medical appointments together

   Your partner will feel supported if you accompany her to as many appointments as you can. This is a great way to learn more about the pregnancy, your partner, and the baby. For example, going to a breastfeeding class or a Lamaze class will teach you how to better support your partner during labor and postpartum.

6. Be present for emotional support

   Your partner will want to talk to you often about her feelings during the pregnancy. She may want to share how active the baby was when you were at work or how she envisions raising the baby. She may also have fears and hopes concerning motherhood that she wants to share with you. At the same time, you will have a lot of these same fears and hopes, making it equally important to share them with her. Pregnancy is a vulnerable time not just for the mother, but also the father. You can both support each other and be there for each other during this time.

Chapter Summary

- The first trimester is when the baby is still in the earliest stages of development.

- As soon as you find out that you and your partner are pregnant, you will both need to book her first prenatal appointment.

- Your first prenatal visit is exceedingly important for the health of your baby.

- Pregnancy is going to take its toll on her physical and mental health, so you will need to be very supportive.

- If you, your partner, or both of you smoke, drink, or take recreational drugs, you must inform the doctor.

- A woman with a healthy pregnancy may still experience some pregnancy complications.

- Paternal support is crucial for a healthy pregnancy and a healthy baby.

In the next chapter you will learn how to prepare for the second trimester of pregnancy.

Chapter Three:

Second Trimester

"Kids put life into perspective. Life happens and you get bad news sometimes, or things don't go your way at work—for me that might mean I lose a game or not play well—but that doesn't affect my mood from day to day. I love going home and seeing the smiles on my daughters' faces being happy to see me, and that makes everything all right."

- Stephen Curry

Known as the "golden period" of pregnancy, the second trimester (week 13 to week 27) is usually the easiest and happiest trimester. During the second trimester, women often don't experience any morning sickness or much tenderness in the breasts. A pregnant woman will also experience less fatigue during the second trimester and will even need less visits to the toilet to urinate, since the fetus has grown out of the pelvic cavity and is no longer pressing on the bladder. Many women feel much more energetic during the second trimester. Spend this time wisely by doing light exercise routines with your partner to keep her healthy and in shape. Even better, after the first trimester, a woman is less likely to miscarry. Week 20 marks the half-way point of the pregnancy. A fetus born on week 24 has a chance of survival in a neonatal intensive care unit. So any early worries should begin to fade away.

By the end of the first trimester, the organs and all the systems will have formed completely. You will notice that the baby will become responsive to outside stimuli in the second trimester. Although the baby's eyelids are still fused shut, if you shine a torch on the mom's stomach, the baby will reflexively move away. Your baby will also feel it if you gently poke the mom's stomach—though you won't feel any movements yet. During these three months, the mother will slowly begin to show that she is carrying. By the beginning of the trimester, the baby is about the size of an apple. By the end of the second trimester, the baby is about the size of a head of cauliflower. The miracle of life will truly start to happen as the baby starts practicing breathing movements and even begins to sleep and wake up in a regular pattern.

The second trimester is also when the mother begins to feel kicks and even jabs (known as quickening). Your baby will start to create a pattern of their own, such as kicking at a particular time or moving a lot when it hears mom's voice. During the next two trimesters, the fetus will now grow rapidly, reaching up to seven times its weight at the end of the first trimester.

Second Trimester Prenatal Visit

As long as the mother does not have any serious complications, there are typically two prenatal visits during the second trimester. The first takes place between weeks 18 and 20 and the second takes place between weeks 24 and 28. The second trimester prenatal visits checks for the mother's:

- Weight

- Urine. A urine test will determine if a pregnant woman has preeclampsia* and hyperglycemia**

- Vitals (such as blood pressure and heart rate)

- Distance from the top of the uterus to her pubic bone, called "fundal height." The fundal height keeps track of the baby's development

* Preeclampsia is a serious condition that results in high blood pressure and excess protein in the mother's urine. It typically occurs anytime between week 20 (the half-way point of a pregnancy) up until six weeks after pregnancy. It typically does not harm your baby, but sometimes leads to premature delivery, breathing problems in newborns, and low birth weight. Symptoms include headaches, sensitivity to light and blurred vision; upper abdominal pain, concentrated on the right side, below the ribs; seizures or convulsions; and swelling on the face, ankles, and upper body.

** Hyperglycemia can refer to gestational diabetes or a woman who suffered with diabetes before pregnancy but was only diagnosed during pregnancy. Uncontrolled or poorly controlled hyperglycemia can lead to macrosomia, i.e., a chubby baby. If a baby becomes too chubby, this presents life-threatening difficulties for both the mother and the baby during pregnancy. Babies with macrosomia may have breathing problems and a higher risk for obesity and type 2 diabetes. They often also suffer dystocia if their shoulders become too big to naturally pass through the birth canal.

These visits will also check for the baby's:

- Heart rate

- Vital organs and body parts. This is done using an anatomy scan, which is a type of ultrasound that checks the baby's body parts and organs, ensuring that they are developing as expected. It verifies that the baby is also at a normal size and that the placenta is correctly positioned. A placenta in the wrong position can be life-threatening for both the mother and the baby.

- Gender (Discuss with your partner beforehand to decide if you would like to know the baby's gender during the checkup.)

- Genetic testing and abnormalities. Noninvasive prenatal testing (NIPT) or amniocentesis is used for this. Also known as cell-free DNA testing, noninvasive prenatal testing analyzes fetal DNA through a sample of the mother's blood. It is commonly used for high-risk women (women above the age of 35 and women with pre-pregnancy health problems or pregnancy-related health complications). For low-risk pregnancies, NIPTs are often inaccurate.

Amniocentesis, on the other hand, is very accurate for determining chromosomal or genetic abnormalities, such as Down syndrome. The medical practitioner will use an ultrasound and a needle to take a small sample of amniotic fluid and produce a picture of the baby's chromosomes. Amniocentesis is invasive and comes with a small risk of miscarriage. It will only be used if your partner has an increased risk of chromosomal and genetic problems.

Questions to Ask Your Doctor

You may have additional or follow-up questions concerning your partner's pregnancy during the second trimester check-ups. Remember to always jot down any questions you think of prior to the check-up. That way, you can ascertain that you don't forget any important questions you may have.

Some questions you may have during the second trimester check-ups include:

- Can I choose who births my baby, such as an obstetrician-gynecologist (MB/GYN), a midwife, or a doula?

- Can you recommend any good pediatricians in the area to register my baby with?

- Besides calling you, what contingency plans should I have in case of an emergency with the mother or the baby?

- It is generally safe to have sex during pregnancy, even during the second trimester when the woman's stomach begins to grow. Can you confirm it is safe for me and my wife based on our personal circumstances?

- Can we travel in the second trimester?

- Is my baby in the right fetal position?

- What type of delivery do you recommend for my partner?

Second Trimester Symptoms

The pregnancy hormone, the chorionic gonadotropin hormone, decreases in the second trimester. Conversely, estrogen and progesterone levels increase to help the fetus grow. Here are some common second trimester symptoms that your partner may experience:

- Braxton Hicks contractions

    These are mild and irregular contractions that typically happen in the afternoon and evening and after physical activity or sex. They will generally stop if your partner moves around or changes position. If they do not stop and the cramps get longer, it could be a symptom of preterm labor, so you will need to contact your doctor immediately.

- Uterus changes

    Your partner's uterus will now reach the height of her belly button. The mother begins to show that she is carrying. As the uterus and stomach grow, the skin on the stomach stretches, causing itching. This may also cause pain on both sides of the body. Moreover, the ligament will begin to stretch to support the uterus causing pain in the lower stomach.

- Increase in appetite

    Despite this increase in appetite, it is not advisable to gain too much weight during pregnancy. A woman with a "normal" BMI should not gain more than 25 - 35 pounds of weight during pregnancy. For underweight women, this figure goes up to 28 - 40 pounds. For overweight women, the figure decreases to 15 - 25 pounds. Finally, for obese women, the figure stays at 10 - 20 pounds. This is why it is recommended that pregnant women do regular light exercises, such as walking, yoga, Pilates, gentle weightlifting, and swimming.

- Back pain

Your partner may begin to experience back pain from weight gain (including the additional weight of the growing fetus).

- Congested nose

    A congested nose and nosebleeds occur as a consequence of the increase in estrogen and progesterone. Blood flow also increases in the second trimester to allow for enough oxygen and nutrients to reach the baby. This also causes nosebleeds and a congested nose because the increased blood flow also affects the mucous membranes and the blood vessels in the nose.

- Leukorrhea

    This is a whitish and odorless vaginal discharge caused by an estrogen imbalance. Leukorrhea is generally safe, however, some vaginal discharges are a symptom of a pregnancy complication. If your partner's vaginal discharge has a foul-smelling odor, is yellow, gray, or green, or is accompanied by swelling, itching and redness around the vaginal area, call your doctor immediately.

- Urinary tract infections

    Urinary tract infections are very common during pregnancy. The symptoms of urinary tract infections include sharp pain while urinating, a strong urgency to urinate immediately, cloudy or smelly urine, and, possibly, fever and back pain. Your partner must see a doctor immediately if she shows symptoms of a UTI. She will be prescribed antibiotics to clear the infection. Left untreated, UTIs can lead to kidney infections.

- Skin pigmentation

    Skin pigmentation occurs because of pregnancy hormones. Your partner may begin to spot brown patches on her face, termed melasma. She may possibly develop a higher sensitivity to the sun and will need to apply plenty of sunscreen. You may also notice a deep dark line stretched between the navel and the pubic hair. This is called Linea nigra.

- Dental issues

  An increase in progesterone and estrogen will cause spongier gums and loose ligaments and bones in your partner's mouth. This may lead to gum bleeding.

- Leg cramps

  The baby begins to place more pressure on your partner's blood vessels and nerves. This will cause leg cramps in her calves. Stretching, hot baths and showers, working out and drinking plenty of water will alleviate her leg cramps.

- Breast Changes

  Your partner will now need to swap to more comfortable sports and maternity bras as her breasts grow bigger and retain some tenderness. The skin around her nipples may also begin to darken. Your partner can use this opportunity to go maternity clothes shopping too because a pregnant woman's stomach grows very quickly, beginning in the second trimester.

- Heartburn

- Constipation

- Indigestion

- Varicose veins

- Hemorrhoids

Preparing for the Baby

Now that you are in the second trimester, you will need to begin preparing for the baby's arrival. It is a great time to start baby proofing your home, ensuring your baby's safety at all times. You will also need to purchase certain home and car equipment for the baby. Do not forget to begin to look for daycares for your baby if you and your partner will be heading back to work after the baby arrives. It can be a long process, so you will benefit greatly from starting the search early.

Finally, you will need to prepare the hospital bag in readiness for your partner's labor.

Babyproofing Your Home

The second trimester is the best time to babyproof your home in preparation for your baby. Since your partner will be much more energetic and comfortable in the second trimester, that may free up some time and energy for you both to babyproof your home.

You may have started to notice how unsafe your home is for a baby. Perhaps you have a coffee table with sharp edges or a swimming pool in your backyard. Despite being comedic, the best tip for babyproofing your home is to crawl around on your hands and knees to check for items, equipment, and other dangerous objects in the house that a crawling baby can reach.

Another tip is to never leave a baby or a toddler alone when they are awake - not even for a minute. A baby can easily suffocate, choke, or fall. Similarly, a toddler can easily pull a heavy object unto themselves or drink a household chemical. Below are some good ways for babyproofing your home in anticipation for your baby.

- Cover all electrical outlets with safety covers.

- Lock away hazardous and toxic products, like cleaning products, in cabinets that cannot be opened or reached. You should also lock away all knives and sharp objects in high cabinets far out of the reach of the baby. Do not leave knives out in the open or in knife block holders, as there is still a possibility the baby can reach them.

- Place clips or locks on containers and outlets that may be within reach.

- Add safety guards on all your windows.

- Add baby gates on all the passageways in the home, as well as at the top and bottom of stairs.

- Put away all the electrical cords so that the baby does not trip over it and or chew on it. It will also prevent you from tripping over cords while holding your baby. For electrical cords out in the open, hide them safely behind furniture.

- Secure all rugs in the home by placing non-slip mats under them.

- Buy a crib and furniture that meets government-approved standards. Make sure they are also built according to these standards.

- Position the crib away from objects and items in the room that can fall on them, such as dressers, lamps, and mirrors.

- Secure all furniture in the house to the wall to prevent heavy items and furniture from falling on the baby.

- Remind yourself and your partner to always unplug and store away appliances that are not in use. For example, you must unplug and put away hot irons and kettles immediately after use to prevent your baby pulling on the cord.

- Leave all furniture bare, removing heavy items and tablecloths. Cover all furniture edges with baby safety padding.

- Place knob covers for your oven/cooker. Always cook on the back hobs, where the baby cannot reach.

- Write down all the numbers you may need to call in an emergency, for example, your pediatrician. Keep physical copies of these numbers and digital back-ups in your phone and on your computer.

- Use curtains and blinds that cannot be reached from a baby's height. Make sure they do not have cords that can be reached by the baby to prevent your infant choking on them.

- Remove tall lamps and unstable objects, like flowerpots, from your home. Keep them in an area that your baby can't access.

- Install carbon monoxide alarms and smoke detectors in every room in your home. Install fire extinguishers in easily accessible positions in your home.

- Buy three first-aid kits. Place one in your baby's room, one in your room and one in the kitchen.

- Consider fire-retardant nighttime clothing and bedsheets for you, your partner, and your baby.

- Buy and install a good quality, government-approved, rear-facing back seat in the back of your car. Place it only in the middle seat then take it for inspection to make sure you have installed it properly.

- Install a baby monitor in your infants room to ensure you can always monitor them.

Prepping the Hospital Bag

The hospital bag is the bag that contains essential birth, labor, and after-birth supplies for mother, father, and baby during their stay at the hospital. Ideally, you should pack two hospital bags to ensure that you don't end up in the hospital without one. Keep one in your car and one in your home or one in your car and one at your place of work etc.

If you can only afford one hospital bag, then leave it in your car at all times. If you have two cars, then leave it in the car that is used more often. The point is, leave the bag packed and ready to go in a location that is easily accessible in case of urgency. There is nothing worse than getting to the hospital and realizing that all of your supplies are still packed away in the garage for example. Consider packing the following items in your hospital bag:

- Parents' photo identification and insurance details.
- Your birth plan, including the contact details of your OB-GYN, midwife, and any of your baby's other medical professionals.
- Money and/or a debit or credit card.
- Your cell phone chargers.
- Newborn baby clothes that will last two weeks in the hospital. At least one of those clothes has to cover the baby's legs so that your newborn can be securely strapped in the baby seat when you take him/her home.
- Baby sling or baby carrier.
- Sunshade for all your car windows. Newborn babies cannot be out in the sun.
- Toiletries, such as toothpaste, shampoo, soap, lotion, and so on, for both parents.

- Enough nightwear and clothes for both parents for a few days. Make sure they are very comfortable clothes and shoes as you both will be very tired.
- Three or so baby blankets.
- Healthy, nutritious, protein-filled snacks and drinks to revive and energize you and your partner.
- Baby formula (in case your baby does not latch onto your partner or if you decide to formula-feed).
- Breast pump, including two bottles and two nipple brushes.
- Comfy pillows for you and your partner.
- Aromatherapy sticks to help you and your partner relax.
- Burp cloths and bibs.
- Nursing bra, breast pads and nursing pillows, and breast pads.
- Lotion for sore nipples.
- Four or five dozen diapers.
- At least two boxes of newborn size diapers (if you are using reusable diapers).
- Changing pad.
- Baby ointment to prevent rashes.
- Disposable wipes or reusable washcloths.
- A handful of pacifiers.
- Baby thermometer.
- Bulb syringe, used for suctioning mucus.
- Eye dropper.
- Medicine spoon.
- Fever medication for the baby.

Chapter Summary

- The second trimester is usually the easiest and happiest trimester.
- Many women feel much more energetic during the second trimester.
- As long as the mother does not have any serious complications, there are typically two prenatal visits during the second trimester.
- During the second trimester, baby proof your home and prepare a hospital bag ready for the birth of your child.

In the next chapter you will learn how to prepare for the third trimester of pregnancy.

Chapter Four:

Third Trimester

"Blessed indeed is the man who hears many gentle voices call him father."

- Lydia Maria Child

During the third trimester (week 28 to week 40), pregnancy usually transpires into a more uncomfortable and painful time once again. The growing baby continues to gain weight and the mother may typically begin to notice more Braxton-Hicks contractions. The weight and ever-changing position of the baby may make your partner unable to get comfortable. Concurrently, emotions may start to run high for you and your partner as the due date nears. Your partner will need to continue light exercise to keep her and the baby healthy.

Furthermore, prenatal visits see a major change during the third trimester. During the third trimester, they increase considerably to bi-weekly visits. This helps your doctor identify any complications and take swift action to handle any concerns if required.

Third Trimester Prenatal Visits

During the third prenatal visits, your doctor will check:

- The growth, development, and position of the fetus.
- Your partner's weight.
- Your partner's blood pressure.
- The fetal heartbeat (the heartbeat of the fetus).
- The height of the fundus (the top of the uterus).
- Preeclampsia, toxemia, or hyperglycemia in your partner's urine. All three conditions can be fatal to your partner and baby. A urine test for albumin and glucose, both of which may indicate the aforementioned conditions.
- Any other symptoms or discomforts noticed by the future mother.

Beginning at approximately week 38, your healthcare practitioner will begin to anticipate the birth of the baby. Your doctor will want to discuss labor and finalize your birth plan. They will also be particularly interested in the mother's contractions. Your doctor may also begin to carry out regular pelvic floor exams to determine the dilation and effacement of the cervix.

Third Trimester Symptoms

- Fatigue

    Your partner will begin to wake up very frequently at night to use the bathroom. This, along with carrying a growing baby and the changes her body has seen in the past six months, will cause her to be fatigued. She will need to relax and sit down very often and will need your help to complete more tasks.

- Edema

    Edema is the swelling of the ankles, hands, and face. It happens as a pregnant woman begins to retain fluid. However, not every pregnant woman in the third trimester will develop this symptom.

- Braxton-Hicks contractions

    These are irregular contractions that start to occur to prepare the woman's body for childbirth.

- Stretch marks

    As the baby grows and the mother's stomach expands, she may begin to see stretch marks on her stomach. Stretch marks may also appear on her breasts, thighs, and buttocks as she gains weight. These are completely normal however, your partner may be really sensitive about them.

- Leg cramps

    Leg cramps will begin to appear more frequently, sometimes even preventing your partner from sleeping at night.

- Decreased libido

    Your partner's sexual libido may also decrease during the third trimester.

- Skin issues

    Skin issues may continue into the third trimester. Skin pigmentation may intensify, causing dark patches of skin on your partner's face to darken even more. The skin on the stomach will also continue to be itchy and dry as it stretches to accommodate the baby.

- Heat Flashes

    Your fetus radiates body heat. Your partner will begin to feel hot from increased skin temperature.

- Increased urinary frequency

    The future mother's increased urinary frequency may now return due to increased pressure being placed on her bladder. As your baby starts to take up more space in your partner's uterus, his/her head may begin pressing down on her bladder. In this case, she may now begin urinating frequently. Equivalently, she may begin to leak urine when she coughs, laughs, sneezes, or exercises.

- Low blood pressure

    The future mother's blood pressure may now decrease as the fetus presses on the main vein that returns blood to her heart.

- Digestive issues

    Your partner may continue to experience constipation, heartburn, and indigestion, if she suffered these symptoms in earlier trimesters.

- Colostrum

    Colostrum is the fluid in your partner's breasts that feeds your baby after birth before milk can be produced. It may begin to leak from your partner's nipples during the third trimester.

- Hair changes

  Hormone stimulation is a symptom of pregnancy. It causes your partner's hair to become coarse and to grow at a faster speed on her arms, legs, and face.

- Leukorrhea

  Leukorrhea, the whitish and odorless vaginal discharge, will increase and may contain more mucus.

- Breast enlargement

  As the future mother starts producing colostrum, her breasts also become enlarged in preparation for the birth.

- Hemorrhoids

  Hemorrhoids may persist from earlier trimesters. In many cases this symptom increases in intensity.

- Shortness of breath

  Your partner's uterus will enlarge in the third trimester until it sits just under her rib cage. As a result, your partner's lungs will have less space to expand, making it difficult to breathe. By propping up her head and shoulders on a pillow while lying down, your partner can breathe deeply into her lungs.

- Backache

  Like many other symptoms, backache may persist from the first and second trimester, increasing in severity in the third trimester as the fetus grows bigger. In the third trimester, your partner may begin to develop sciatica, a very painful condition where nerve pain travels from the lower back to her glutes and legs. This could be because of the baby pressing on a sciatic nerve or because of hormonal changes. Give your partner plenty of lower back massages to help relieve the pain. She can also practice daily yoga and physical therapy.

- Loss of balance

Your partner may suffer a loss of balance because of the extra weight now resting in her abdomen.

- Varicose veins

Varicose veins may typically appear in the first trimester and may increase in severity in the third trimester.

Signs that Your Partner Is in Labor

The third trimester will typically end with labor and/or birth. You will need to be able to spot some of the signs of labor as they happen so that you will know when to take your partner to the hospital.

- Dilation

Dilation occurs when your partner's cervix begins to open in preparation for birth. It is a natural way to track how labor is progressing in the mother. During active labor, the mother's dilation progresses very quickly, beginning at 0 cm and concluding at 10 cm. At 10cm, the mother is ready to give birth to the baby.

Think of the uterus as a balloon. The cervix is the neck and opening of the balloon. Filling the balloon up with air causes the neck of the balloon to draw up and open wider because of the pressure of the air. Similarly, the cervix draws up and opens wider to create room for the baby to push through the uterus.

- Effacement

Effacement occurs when the cervix softens, shortens, and thins to the size of a sheet of paper, allowing for the baby to pass through. It can be uncomfortable for a woman in labor and usually causes women to feel irregular but mild contractions. Some women, on the other hand, feel nothing. Nonetheless, vaginal delivery is not possible until a woman is 100 percent effaced.

- Vaginal Discharge

Typically occurring anytime between a few days before labor or just before labor, a woman in labor will see an increase in vaginal discharge, ranging from clear to pink to bloody.

- Baby Drops

A baby will drop usually up to a few weeks to a few hours before labor begins. The baby drops lower into the abdomen, changing the way in which your partner carries the baby.

- Nesting

Nesting is a very quaint sign of upcoming labor because it is instinctual. Despite women in the third trimester feeling lethargic and fatigued, nesting is characterized by a sudden increase in a woman's energy levels. During nesting, the mother begins to prepare her home for the arrival of her baby frantically and energetically. This is the same instinct in birds that causes them to build a nest for their soon-to-be-laid eggs.

If you notice your partner is suddenly filled with an energetic preoccupation to prepare the house for the baby, this is a sign that labor is approaching.

- Water Breaks

This is the best-known sign of labor; once your partner's membranes rupture, her water breaks.

- Regular Contractions

Unlike Braxton-Hicks contractions, regular contractions are a sign that a woman is in labor. A regular contraction is defined as a contraction that gets closer and stronger every time. They usually last between 30 to 70 seconds and don't stop until childbirth begins.

Three Stages of Labor

There are three easily distinguishable stages of labor. They are:

1. **Stage One**: Also known as the latent phase, stage one is the cervix "warming up" in preparation for birth. If this is your partner's first pregnancy, the latent phase will very likely take longer than usual. Her contractions will be mild and irregular as her cervix effaces to prepare for birth.

   The latent phase is when you dilate from 0 cm to 6 cm. The active phase is when your cervix begins to dilate rapidly.

2. **Stage Two**: Also known as the active phase, stage two begins when a woman's cervix is fully dilated to 10 centimeters. Even after a mother reaches cervical dilation, the baby is not ready for birth until s/he has moved all the way down the birth canal. A mother cannot begin to push until this occurs.

   Once the baby is delivered, stage two has concluded. If this is your partner's first pregnancy, pushing will typically take longer. Similarly, it will also take longer if she has had an epidural. During birth, pushing can only occur during contractions. After every contraction pause (occurring every 2 to 3 minutes apart and lasting between 60 to 90 seconds) the mother must rest.

3. **Stage Three**: This is the stage where the mother delivers the placenta. Remember that the placenta is formed to help feed the

baby oxygen and nutrients and transport waste away from the fetus. Without a baby, the mother does not need a placenta. As such, her body will reject it through the same contractions with which it expelled the baby.

This is the shortest stage of labor, lasting only between 5 to 30 minutes.

If you are worried about symptoms that your partner is showing during the third trimester, do not hesitate to call for your doctor. Catching complications early gives your baby and your partner a greater chance of returning to health quickly.

Fetal Development

During the third trimester, the fetus increases in size and weight. By week 40 (the end of the third trimester), the fetus will weigh 6 to 9 pounds on average. It will also measure between 19 to 21 inches.

Fetal development during the third trimester includes:

- Between weeks 38 to 40, the fetus will flip over, positioning itself head down to prepare for birth. It is around this time that lightening will occur. Lightening is the process whereby the baby's head drops into the pelvic area, "engaged" for birth. If lightening does not occur, your doctor will discuss with you the different methods for managing it.

- The skull of the fetus will stay soft in preparation for birth. Soft skull bones allow for the fetus to pass through the birth canal easier.

- The lanugo (the protective soft, downy hair on the fetus' skin) will have mostly fallen off in preparation for birth. You may notice patches of it on the baby's shoulders after birth. However, this will also soon fall off post-birth.

- The fetus will now be able to see and hear, ready for the outside world.

- During the third trimester, the brain will now begin its final stages of development. Similarly, the lungs and kidneys will continue to mature.

- The fetus has now developed the ability to cry. In addition, the fetus can now suck its thumb in the uterus.

- The baby is coated in vernix caseosa. This is the white, creamy coating on the baby's skin that serves to protect it from the amniotic fluid. If a fetus' skin comes into contact with the amniotic fluid, it chaps, hardens, and develops abrasions.

What if My Partner Is Overdue?

It is very common for a pregnant woman to go into labor before or after her due date. This is because the due date is only an estimate of the birth, not an accurate prediction of your child's due date. Indeed, 30% of pregnant women usually give birth after their due date, while less than 5% of pregnant women give birth on their exact due date.

If your partner is still pregnant by week 42, she will be considered overdue. At this point, your doctor will become involved, monitoring your partner to make sure the baby is healthy. Usually, your doctor will carry out an ultrasound (biophysical profile) on your partner to check that the baby is not showing any signs of complications. Your doctor will carry out a nonstress test, which checks your baby's heart rate. Alternatively, your baby's amniotic fluid volume may be assessed to ensure that your baby is not in any danger. Low amniotic fluid, known as oligohydramnios, may compress the umbilical cord during contractions, causing serious health risks for your baby.

Your doctor will also ask the mother about the baby's movements. Your partner will be instructed to count the baby's kick count. If there is any inconsistency or decrease in the baby's kick count, you and your partner will have to alert your doctor immediately. This is because pregnancy that extends past 41 weeks poses health risks for your baby. These health risks increase once the pregnancy extends past 41 weeks and 6 days (a late-term pregnancy) and 42 weeks (a post term pregnancy). Apart from oligohydramnios, your baby is at risk for fetal macrosomia, which, during delivery, can lead to shoulder dystocia.

Additionally, a late pregnancy also increases your baby's chance of post maturity syndrome. This is when your baby begins to experience developmental stages that should occur post-birth. Since your baby remains in the uterus past the post term, it will begin to lose fat under the skin, significantly lose the vernix caseosa and have the first bowel movement (meconium) inside the amniotic sac. When meconium contaminates the amniotic fluid, it can cause your baby to breathe in the contaminated fluid, causing meconium aspiration syndrome.

Late term and post term birth also pose risks of complications for the mother, including infection, severe vaginal tear, and postpartum bleeding. Women who are more likely to experience post term pregnancy are usually women who:

- Are first-time pregnant mothers.

- Are carrying a male baby.

- Have previously experienced a post term pregnancy.

- Are obese (i.e., with a body mass index of 30 or above).

- Have their due date miscalculated (typically because of uncertainty over the exact date of the start of their last menstrual period or, usually, if their due date was calculated based on a late second- or third-trimester ultrasound).

By week 41, your doctor will discuss labor induction with you if your partner's placenta is no longer providing enough nutrients and oxygen for the baby. This is another complication of late term and post term pregnancy, wherein the baby becomes too big to be nourished and kept alive through the placenta. If, after all the checks, your doctor determines your baby is fine, labor will not be induced at this stage. This is because inducing labor comes with its own health risks and complications for both mother and baby.

By week 42, if the baby has not arrived, your doctor will seriously ask you to consider inducing labor. If you, your partner, and your doctor decide to induce pregnancy, your partner may be given medication to ripen her cervix. Your OB-GYN/midwife may also dilate your partner's cervix. This procedure is carried out by inserting a small catheter into her cervix with an inflatable balloon attached on the end. The doctor then fills the balloon with saline and rests it against the inside of the cervix. If after this, the amniotic sac is still intact, your doctor may use a thin plastic hook to break your partner's water by creating an opening in the sac.

If needed, your healthcare practitioner may also prescribe your partner with contraction-inducing medication.

Prolonging your pregnancy after week 42 also comes with its own complications, including a lack of nutrients and oxygen for your baby, stillbirth, and difficulties delivering a larger baby. Healthcare professionals, in general, do not recommend this.

Preparing for the Baby

You will have done most of the preparation for your baby in the first and second trimester. There are a few other things you should do during this time to prepare for the baby coming home.

- Wash all your baby clothes and sheets and put them away before use.

- Stock up on essentials to last a month or two, like toiletries, household supplies and newborn supplies. You should avoid taking your baby out (unless it is very important) until s/he receives pivotal vaccines in month 1 or 2.

- Prepare healthy, nutritious meals for you and your partner for the next month or so. The new baby will keep both of you very busy. Moreover, your partner will need regular, nutritious meals to help her body heal from the nine months of pregnancy and, if breastfeeding, to help produce nutritious milk for the baby.

- If available through your occupation, consider taking paternity leave.

- Call all of your utility companies and set all your bills on automatic payments. Get your finances to run on automatic for the next few months. You will be too tired and too busy to remember anything during the first few months. This system prevents you from forgetting to pay a bill.

Preparing for Breastfeeding

If your partner plans to breastfeed, you will need to prepare for it before labor. You will need to tell your midwife or OB-GYN that she has chosen to breastfeed. This way, the delivery room staff can support her after the baby is born.

Many hospitals now have lactation consultants to help you if you encounter any problems with lactation postpartum. Likewise, the delivery room staff will aid your partner in forming a close bond with your baby after birth. They will also help your partner if the baby is having difficulties with latching onto your partner's breasts for food.

If your partner is not able to breastfeed for any health reasons, your OB-GYN will be able to let her know beforehand. There are many reasons why a mother might not be able to breastfeed, including breast implants, supplements, medication, breast surgery, recreational drug use, history of medical problems and infections, and cancer treatments, among others.

You and your partner may also ask your healthcare practitioner for referrals to local breastfeeding classes.

Chapter Summary

- During the third trimester prenatal visits will become bi-weekly.

- You will need to be able to spot some of the signs of labor as they happen so that you will know when to take your partner to hospital.

- If you are worried about symptoms that your partner is showing during the third trimester, do not hesitate to call your doctor.

- Catching complications early gives your baby and your partner a greater chance of returning to health quickly.

- By week 42, if the baby has not arrived, your doctor will seriously ask you to consider inducing labor.

In the next chapter you will learn how to take care of your baby postpartum.

Chapter Five:

Postpartum, Taking Care Of Your Baby

"As fathers, we need to be involved in our children's lives not just when it's convenient or easy, and not just when they're doing well—but when it's difficult and thankless, and they're struggling. That is when they need us most."

- Barack Obama

Leaving the hospital with your baby can be one of the most amazing, joyful, and daunting experiences of your life. You are now a father. In your hands lies a life that will depend on you for nearly everything until s/he reaches adulthood. You are now responsible not just for your baby's physical health, but also mental health, emotional health, and every other developmental milestone for the ongoing future!

However, for your baby to reach adulthood, you will need to take the greatest of care for the next two years, which are the most important developmental period of an infant's life, barring prepartum.

Now that you have brought the baby (or babies) home, knowing how to take care of her/him, as well as your partner, is the key to postpartum success.

Week One Development & Milestones

- Your baby can lift her/his head for just a few seconds when laying on his/her stomach.

- Your baby will need 14-17 hours of sleep daily to recover from childbirth. During this time, your baby's body, organs, and brain will be developing rapidly.

- The eyesight of a newborn is still developing after birth. At week one, your baby can focus on you when you are between 8-12 feet in front of him/her.

- Newborns can recognize voices they heard while in the womb. Talk to your newborn often. This practice will comfort your baby.

- Newborns also have irregular breath and may sometimes stop breathing for seconds at a time.

- Your baby's body is developing new skills needed in the outside world. These are skills that your baby did not need to survive in the uterus, such as sucking and digesting.

- Your baby's body will begin to develop its own individualized set of microbes. These microbes will make up a big part of his/her immune system.

Week One Care

- Newborns must always be placed on their back; never put them on their stomach or on their side.

- You must make every effort to never sleep in the same bed as your baby. You may accidentally roll over onto your baby during sleep, which could be fatal for your baby. Instead, place your baby's cradle or crib right next to your bed.

- The mattress in your baby's crib or bed must be very firm. You should also use fitted sheets to avoid the danger of suffocation.

- Give your baby his/her first bath during week one. Wrap your baby delicately in a baby towel. Unwrap portions of your baby's body and gently wash the area with a soft baby sponge or washcloth dipped in water and baby soap. Pat your baby gently to dry him/her afterwards.

- Spend as much time giving your baby skin-to-skin contact as possible. Newborns are happier and develop better when given skin-to-skin contact.

- Expect your baby to wake up every 2-4 hours for feeding.

- Feed your baby every two to four hours. Your baby will feed between 8-12 times a day. Your baby will begin to gain weight after day four. If your baby is not gaining weight after day four, s/he is not being fed enough. (Monitor your baby's weight carefully in the first two months. If your baby is not gaining enough weight, you should speak to your pediatrician).

- Allow your baby to eat as much food as possible if breastfeeding. In general, your baby will eat between 16 to 24 ounces of breastmilk or formula per day.

- Your baby will need to develop arm, back, leg, and back muscles to crawl, sit, roll over and walk. Tummy time is a great way for your baby to develop his/her muscles. For newborns over one week old, practice tummy time two to three times a day for three to five minutes per session. For newborns under one-week-old, tummy time should last one to three minutes, three times a day. Your baby will be more responsive to it if you do it when s/he is very comfortable, usually after a diaper change or a nap.

Taking Care of Yourself

Don't let yourself get too tired. Your baby is waking up to feed between 8-12 times a day, including at night. Being too fatigued can cause you to make mistakes or put your baby's life in jeopardy. Ensure that you are sleeping every time your baby is sleeping. Take turns with your partner to feed your baby (if you are formula-feeding) and take care of her/him. This allows both of you to get deep sleep every 24 hours. If your partner is breastfeeding, spend time keeping the house in order, doing chores, drawing her baths, massaging her, and helping to keep her as comfortable as possible.

Most women do not recover fully from pregnancy, labor, and childbirth until at least a year after birth.

Your partner might be sad in the first few days postpartum. This is a normal symptom, known as "baby blues," that affects 80% of postpartum women. It is usually the result of hormonal fluctuations that occur during pregnancy and during and after childbirth, as well as sleep deprivation. Your partner needs time to settle into a new reality that the baby is finally here. Baby blues is not postpartum depression. Baby blues typically ends after week two, while postpartum depression typically lasts for a much longer time, especially if left untreated.

Symptoms of baby blues include anxiety, insomnia, crying spells, feeling overwhelmed, mood swings, appetite issues, reduced concentration and sadness.

Watch out for symptoms of postpartum depression in your partner. They are:

- Withdrawing from her friends and family
- Loss of appetite or overeating
- Insomnia or oversleeping
- Loss of energy; fatigue/lethargy
- Depressed mood; severe mood swings
- Intense anxiety; intense panic attacks
- Inability to bond with the newborn
- Recurrent thoughts of suicide or death
- Excessive crying
- Restlessness
- Thoughts of harming the baby or harming herself
- Little to no interest in formerly pleasurable activities
- Intense anger; intense irritability
- Hopelessness; fearing not being a good parent
- Feelings of worthlessness, inadequacy, shame, or guilt
- Inability to think clearly, make decisions, or concentrate

If you notice these symptoms, speak to your partner about seeking professional help. Fathers can also suffer from postpartum depression. Between 4% and 25% of fathers deal with postpartum depression within the first two months of a baby's birth. It is likely that a father can develop the mood disorder from the mother who is also struggling with it.

Research (Kim & Swain, 2007) on paternal postpartum depression (PPD) states that:

"Paternal PPD has high comorbidity with maternal PPD and might also be associated with other postpartum psychiatric disorders. Paternal PPD has negative impacts on family, including increasing emotional and behavioral problems among their children (either directly or through the mother) and increasing conflicts in the … relationship. Changes in hormones, including testosterone, estrogen, cortisol, vasopressin, and prolactin, during the postpartum period in fathers may be biological risk factors in paternal PPD. Fathers who have ecological risk factors, such as excessive stress from becoming a parent, lack of social supports for parenting, and feeling excluded from mother-infant bonding, may be more likely to develop paternal PPD."

If you or your partner (or both of you) are experiencing symptoms of PPD, especially thoughts of harming yourself or harming your child, put your baby in a safe place, or ask a family, neighbor, or friend to take the baby, then call either your doctor or the organizations below immediately.

National Hopeline Network	1-800-SUICIDE (1-800-784-2433)
National Strategy for Suicide Prevention: LifeLine	1-800-273-TALK (1-800-273-8255)
Postpartum Support International	(800) 944-4PPD or (800) 944-4773
PPDMoms	1-800-PPD MOMS (1-800-773-6667)

Weeks Two-Four Development & Milestones

- Your baby will begin to show signs of hunger, such as clenched fists, hands in mouth, smacking or licking lips, and turning their head towards the bottle or your partner's breasts. Do not wait until your baby is crying before you feed them. A baby is usually hungry a long while before they begin crying, so learn to become aware of these signs. If your baby begins to cry from hunger, s/he may get too frustrated and refuse to eat, further causing more tears and unhappiness.

- When your baby is full, signs indicating this include a closed mouth, turning the head away from the bottle or your partner's breasts, and relaxed fists.

- You can now distinguish different reasons why your baby is crying.

  - A hungry baby will have a repetitive, low-pitched cry.

  - A tired or uncomfortable baby will cry without stopping, intensifying the cry the longer it goes.

  - A sick baby will whimper softly, unable to put much strength into crying.

  - An overstimulated baby will be very fussy and almost angry, as the baby moves away from the stimuli.

  - A baby with colic will wail. Colic is a condition that is common among newborns. It is defined by a baby crying for three to four hours a day without stopping, for at least three to four days a week. It is theorized that babies develop colic because they are struggling to adjust to the world outside of the womb.

- In week two, your newborn goes through a growth spurt and needs plenty of food, sleep, and comfort.

- Your baby will grow by about 1.5-2 inches by the end of week four.

- Your baby's vision, reflexes, and muscle movements are also improving by the end of week four.

- Your baby's sleep time will increase to 16-18 hours a day.

Weeks Two-Four Care

- If breastfeeding, your baby will be eating every 2-3 hours in week two because it is still in a growth spurt. If formula-fed, your baby will be eating every 4-5 hours. A newborn is growing very fast and should be allowed to feed whenever they demand. By week four, your baby's feeding will very likely slow down. Simply follow the golden rule of feeding your baby whenever s/he demands and making sure you don't stop feeding until s/he rejects the food. Breastfed babies will need to be given vitamin D3 supplements. Speak to your pediatrician about this.

- Your baby will need to go for his/her first pediatrician's appointment in week two. Always take your baby's chart with you to all pediatrician appointments. The chart will contain important information about your baby's development and medical history. The first visit checks that your baby's brain, reflexes, and nervous system are developing correctly.

- To soothe a baby with colic, check the usual causes of a fussy baby, such as indigestion, gas, a soiled diaper, hunger, temperature, and comfort. If your baby is still crying after you have made these adjustments, hold your baby skin-to-skin to soothe him/her. Similarly, you can take your baby for a walk in a baby carrier or sling. The fresh air and new sights, coupled with very close and warm contact with you, may have a soothing effect. This may comfort and lull your baby to sleep. A baby carrier or sling also enables your baby to hear your heartbeat and your voice, further soothing your baby.

- The umbilical cord will fall off by week three. Keep it dry to make the process faster. If you need to wipe blood or other secretions around the area, use a washcloth or cotton swab dipped in water and, if necessary, soap. Pat dry immediately after.

- Once the umbilical cord falls off, give your baby his/her first bath. Use a baby bath or a kitchen sink. If you use a kitchen sink, add some towels on the bottom to prevent slipping. For the bath, you will need:

    - A baby washcloth
    - Lukewarm water
    - A small cup to wash the baby's head and body
    - A baby hairbrush
    - A baby towel
    - Baby body wash

To bathe your baby:

- Using your wrist, check that the water is lukewarm.
- Fill up the sink or tub four inches full.
- Wash your baby gently using the washcloth and body wash.
- Gently wash your baby's hair using the hairbrush.

- Rinse your baby's body and hair slowly and lightly using the cup.
- Tightly wrap your baby in the towel, then oil his/her skin and hair.

Other activities:

- Watch out for flat head syndrome or plagiocephaly. Flat head syndrome occurs when a baby is left too long on its back. A baby's skull is very soft and will begin to flatten at the back in this case. Carry your baby often to reduce time spent lying on his/her back.
- Massage your newborn to help him/her relax, prevent indigestion, soothe colic, and help your baby sleep better, thereby helping your baby grow. It will also help you bond with your baby as it improves your baby's coordination, muscle tone, immune system, and skin texture. Massage your baby with baby lotion when s/he is most comfortable, calm and alert, such as after bath time. Keep the room warm and relaxing and speak to your baby as you massage. Massage your baby's limbs, moving from the top to the bottom. Then massage your baby's stomach to aid digestion, stroking from the lower right side of your baby's belly to the lower left side.

Taking Care of Yourself

Continue to check in with your partner regularly to make sure that you are both okay. Eat healthy, nutritious meals with plenty of nuts, seeds, fruits, vegetables, and low-mercury fish. Sleep when the baby is asleep and take turns leaving the baby with the other so you can spend time alone doing stress-relieving activities such as exercising and meditation.

Weeks Five-Eight Development & Milestones

- Your infant will now start sleeping for longer periods at night, allowing him/her to be more alert in the daytime.

- Your infant will now sleep for around 16 hours per day.

- Your baby will make baby sounds, like "coo" as s/he tries to talk.

- Your infant will begin socially smiling at you by week 6.

- S/he will be practicing hand-eye coordination and will start grabbing at objects. A soft toy and a play gym will help your baby develop this skill further.

- By week 8, your baby will start to try rolling over from the tummy to the back.

- Your baby will begin to have approximately one bowel movement a day because his/her body is absorbing as much nutrients as it can from the formula and/or breast milk.

- Your baby will start to recognize your face and the faces of people s/he sees regularly. They love to study human faces at this point and will stare at you or your partner for long periods of time.

- Your infant will start to cry if bored. Take your baby on walks and play with your baby with age-appropriate toys to prevent boredom.

- Take part in activities that will help you bond with your baby. Dance with him/her, bouncing your baby softly. Play with your baby every day and cradle him/her every day while maintaining eye contact. Soothe your baby when s/he is upset and even make silly faces to entertain him/her. These activities will cause your baby to associate feeling good with you.

- Look out for signs of constipation in your baby. Your baby's stool should be loose and soft. If it is hard and resembles pellets then this is a sign of a constipated baby. A constipated baby may also show discomfort and irritability when having a bowel movement.

- You will need to take your baby in for a two-month check-up. Here, you can ask your pediatrician any questions you may have. This is when your baby will also receive the first round of vaccines, consisting of polio, hepatitis B, TaP (diphtheria, tetanus, and pertussis), Hib (for meningitis) and the rotavirus vaccines. Your baby can be given a topical anesthetic an hour before receiving the injections.

Weeks Five-Eight Care

- If your partner is heading back to work in the second month, you will need to make the transition to bottle feeding. This way, your partner can pump breast milk and store it for the baby's feed when she is not around. After pumping, breast milk stays safe for 6 hours at room temperature; 24 hours in a cooler with ice packs; 5 to 8 days in a refrigerator; 2 weeks in a freezer compartment in the fridge; 3 to 4 months in a separate freezer; and 6 to 12 months in a deep freezer.

- To make the transition from breast milk to bottle milk, you will need to make sure that someone else feeds your baby, not your partner. You can do this. If your partner bottle feeds your baby for the first time, your baby will be confused and cranky and may take longer to make the transition because they can see, smell, and feel mom but are not being breastfed as they are used to.

Secondly, during transitions, feed your baby in the early morning when s/he is alert, refreshed and energized from the night's sleep. You may not be successful in coaxing your baby to try a bottle the first few times, so do not be disappointed if this happens.

- Your baby may have acid reflux regularly. This is normal. Avoid overfeeding your baby; burp her/him regularly; don't play or do any physical activity with your baby immediately after food; and don't place pressure on your baby's tummy after feeding.

- Feeding should continue as before. That is, feed your baby as much as s/he needs before she rejects the bottle or breast and feed your baby whenever s/he is hungry. If your baby finishes a bottle, offer another one until s/he rejects it. If your baby finishes the milk in one breast, your partner should offer the second one until the baby indicates that s/he is full.

- Tummy time can progress up to 10 to 15 minutes per session at this point and s/he should gradually be getting stronger.

- Always keep your baby's bottom very clean, dry, and moisturized before diapering. This prevents diaper rash. Use rash cream or ointment to keep it moisturized and always change your baby's diapers immediately after it is soiled or every two hours, if unsoiled.

- Start creating bedtime rituals that will signify to your baby that it is time for bed. Things like a bath, a massage, turning on a fan, a lullaby or bedtime story can all be used to create rituals. Keep your bedtime rituals consistent. Do not feed your baby as a bedtime ritual. Your baby is starting to fall into his/her sleep rhythms in month two. Feeding times can vary and can work against the routine you're trying to create.

- If your infant's nose is stuffy, use a saline drop to clear away irritants. Your baby will sneeze a lot in early infancy because their respiratory system is still sensitive to irritants in the air.

- For a runny nose, use a saltwater nasal drop and a nasal aspirator to clear the nasal passages. Watch out for a high fever paired with a runny nose. This is a sign your baby needs to see the pediatrician immediately. If symptoms of a runny nose do not decrease after a week, call your pediatrician.

- If your baby has watery eyes once in a while, don't worry. It is just a blocked tear duct. This is normal and will fix itself. However, if you see signs of infection around the eye, call your pediatrician immediately.

Taking Care of Yourself

Continue to check in with your partner regularly to make sure that you are both okay. Once your baby gets his/her first vaccines, you can introduce the rest of your family and friends. You can also enlist their help to watch your baby once in a while so you can get some much-needed sleep and quality time with your partner.

It is common to feel as though you are abandoning your baby once you head back to work. Don't let this get you down. This is a common feeling that will only set you back if you let it. Instead, concentrate on what you can do to help your baby, from working to provide financially to spending as much time as you can with him/her when you are not at work. Lastly, if possible, you may speak to your boss about working remotely, whether full-time or part-time.

Chapter Summary

- The first two years of your baby's life are the most important developmental period of a person's life, barring prepartum.

- Don't let yourself get too tired. Ensure that you are sleeping every time your baby is sleeping.

- Your partner might be sad in the first few days postpartum. This is normal. It is known as "baby blues."

- Watch out for symptoms of postpartum depression in yourself and your partner.

- It is common to feel as though you are abandoning your baby once you head back to work. Don't let this get you down.

Conclusion

"Dads are most ordinary men turned by love into heroes, adventures, story-tellers, and singers of songs."

— Pam Brown

Becoming a father is no easy challenge. Most men will tell you that it is the most difficult yet most rewarding accomplishment of their lives.

You are just getting started. You are taking a step that billions of men have taken before you and billions more will. By reading this book, you have set yourself on the path of becoming a good father. You have displayed a willingness to learn, to be compassionate, selfless, emotionally intelligent, emotionally open, and supportive. These are qualities that make a great father!

The first twelve months of pregnancy gives you the opportunity to practice these skills in preparation for not just the next few decades, but the remainder of your life. Any father worth his salt will tell you that fatherhood never ends no matter how old your children become.

Do not be afraid to make a decision or take action because of the fear of making mistakes. All parents make many mistakes along the way. Your child will be happy, healthy, and loved not when you never make mistakes, but when you make yourself eager to correct your mistakes and never repeat them. This book has brought you all the important information that you need to know to ensure that you don't make big mistakes that might affect your fetus' and, later, infant's development. In which case, you really don't have to worry. You've got this!

Finally, don't be afraid to continue to seek therapy, if you feel you would benefit from it. Whether it be couples therapy or individual therapy, remember that a happy, well-rounded child has happy, well-rounded parents.

www.ingramcontent.com/pod-product-compliance
Lightning Source LLC
Chambersburg PA
CBHW071750080526
44588CB00013B/2208